WHY FREE CHURCH MINISTRY?

WHY FREE CHURCH MINISTRY?

Serving God in the Independent Church

Graham Beynon

10 Publishing
a division of 10 of those.com

First published in Great Britain in 2015

British Library Cataloguing in Publication Data
A record for this book is available from the British Library

ISBN: 978-1-910587-49-2

Designed by Diane Warnes

Printed in the UK by CPI

10Publishing, a division of 10ofthose.com
Unit C, Tomlinson Road, Leyland, PR25 2DY, England
Email: info@10ofthose.com
Website: www.10ofthose.com

CONTENTS

SERIES INTRODUCTION

The Hub Conference was launched by the Fellowship of Independent Evangelical Churches (FIEC) as an annual conference to help men and women find clear routes into Independent church ministry. For those 'just looking' as well as those 'just started', 'The Hub' supports and equips them in their journey through training and into gospel ministry.

Led by experienced gospel workers from the FIEC, and supported by leaders from colleges and courses, The Hub Conference provides Bible ministry and a wide range of seminars on ministry-related issues. Out of that conference this series of books was born. It's designed to resource people in many areas of Christian work and for a lifetime of ministry.

Someone once described theological books as 'a "college of teachers" committed to helping you do your best to handle the Word of truth'. We hope this series will play a small but significant part in that library of wisdom, at whatever stage you find yourself.

We hope that these books will also be a great help to pastors and leaders, not only in providing a refresher, but also to equip those you are discipling in your congregation for leadership and ministry.

In this next book in the series, Graham Beynon helps us think through the reasons for choosing not only to train, but also to serve in free church ministry. As someone who is both a pastor of a free church and Director of Independent Ministry Training at Oak Hill College, Graham is well placed to do just that.

Whether you come from an Independent church background or not, this book will hopefully show and persuade you of the value of free church ministry.

Trevor Archer and Dan Green
Series editors

fiec

the FELLOWSHIP of INDEPENDENT EVANGELICAL CHURCHES

INTRODUCTION

In my late twenties I was considering going into full-time church ministry. I had been brought up in the United Reformed Church, but then had come to faith in an evangelical Anglican church. While at university I had gone to an independent church purely on the basis that the Bible was taught well there. I then was in a Baptist church mainly because of some personal influence. But which church should I plan to work in looking ahead to the future?

That was a significant question. It affected decisions on training in the short term, and then ministry in the future. I realised a number of factors came into play:

- My instinctive reactions: how did I feel about the different churches I had been in, and what was my impression of the denominations or groups they belonged to?
- Personal factors: my wife had grown up in independent churches and was very unsure about my going into Anglican ministry. Meanwhile my brother and various friends had gone into the Anglican Church.
- Theological issues: what did I believe about baptism and church government, and should

such things make any difference to where I would minister?

I came to realise that while the instinctive reactions and personal factors were significant, they should not be determinative. Actually, I should decide what my convictions were about the theological issues and choose a church grouping that best sat with those convictions. For me, eventually, that meant choosing free church ministry.

It's important to be clear that such issues are not the heart of gospel ministry – which is about teaching God's word and loving people – but are still significant within gospel ministry. Consider the following questions:

- Where does authority lie in the local church?
- How should churches be led?
- How should decisions be made?
- Who decides whether someone can belong to a church?
- What does, or should, membership of a church involve?
- How would a leader be removed from a church if they became heretical?
- Should a member be removed from a church if they are consistently immoral, and if so, how should that happen?

Gospel ministry in a church is always embedded in a context, and this list of issues form significant parts of that context. Some of them are more background related, whereas others connect more directly with church life, but they all play a part in shaping the context and nature of ministry.

Consider the analogy of family life. How you make decisions, whether you all eat together, who does which chores and so on do not make up the heart of life as a family. But they are part of the context for life together as a family and some of them significantly influence that life. So it is with churches. And therefore those considering church ministry need to decide which context they will work in.

This small book is written for those in a similar position to me all those years ago. You may have a background in different churches as I did or you might feel a strong instinct towards, or away from, different denominations. Recognise the significance of those factors, but try not to let them rule the day. Grow in your convictions as to what God teaches about church life and let that shape your decision.

To help with that I want to explain what free church ministry is, the biblical basis for it, its history, and how free churches work in practice; then we'll finish with some advantages and pitfalls. I am of course biased.

I write as someone who has come to free church convictions. I will do my best to discuss the issues even-handedly but you may want to read something from another perspective as well. I hope, though, that what is written here will help you decide where to serve the Lord Jesus.

WHAT IS FREE CHURCH MINISTRY?

The first thing we should do in thinking about why you might choose free church ministry is answer the question 'What is free church ministry?' And that's harder than you might think because one of the results of being 'free' is that you can be anything! So 'free churches' can vary widely from each other.

As we'll see later, the key driving force for the creation of free churches was the desire to organise church life according to biblical principles. Of course this desire was expressed by people who thought that the established church of the day *wasn't* currently organised by those principles.

INDEPENDENT ORGANISATION AND MINISTRY

So at the heart of free church ministry is the 'freedom' to obey the Bible in church life. That is, it gives freedom from an institutional structure which dictates elements of church life. So, for example, a church within the Church of England *has* to have a Parochial Church Council, church wardens and so on as part of its leadership. Those working in such structures may be very happy with that, or they may prefer that was not the case yet have their own way of working within these confines. But the point of free church ministry is that it is free from such confines.

So first, free church ministry is the freedom to organise churches as we think the Bible describes it. Leadership, church structures, decision-making, membership, exercise of discipline and more are all thought through from Scripture (hopefully with a healthy respect for past tradition). As we said above, this freedom has a knock-on effect: different ideas of what the Bible teaches about these areas leads to differences between free churches. But the point is that they are free to decide them.

Second, free church ministry means the freedom to exercise ministry in your setting as you think is most appropriate and helpful. That might mean employing certain staff members or starting new ministries such as a church plant. By comparison, in some institutional churches, permission from elsewhere is needed for such things – and may not always be granted. So free church ministry brings the freedom to decide the best way to minister where you are.

We can bring these two ideas together if we think of free churches as 'independent':

1. They are independent in their *church structures* – no human authority outside the local church tells them how to run themselves.

2. They are independent in their *church ministry* – no outside group tells them what decisions they may make.

INDEPENDENCE NOT FREEDOM

It is important to say what free church ministry is *not* as well. It is not (or at least should not be) freedom from relationships with other churches. Free churches are independent in their government, but they should never be isolationist in their mindset. They are free to take part in local or national networks as they see fit and should have a concern for other churches and partnership with them. For many free churches in the UK this is expressed in being part of the FIEC as a national network, and often in belonging to a regional Gospel Partnership as well as other local networks.

Free church ministry is also not freedom from authority. Some have assumed that free churches are anti-authoritarian because of their independent set-up. That should not be the case. Rather the concern is to submit to the authority of the Lord Jesus. As we will see later, early nonconformists separated from the established church precisely because they wanted to bow to Jesus in every area of church life.

Lastly, free church ministry is not freedom to look down on brothers and sisters in institutional church structures. Those in free churches may well believe they have a more biblically based church structure, but these brothers and sisters serve the same Lord Jesus, and do so in good conscience. Plus, while issues of church government are important, they are still secondary to the gospel which unites us.

So while free churches vary, this is what they share in common: independence in church government and ministry.

THE BIBLICAL BASIS FOR FREE CHURCHES

The argument for free church ministry begins with the biblical description of churches. It is important to recognise these arguments fall into two categories. Some of them are for free churches themselves: that is, for the independence of the local church from wider structures. Other arguments, however, are for a style of church or leadership structure that could exist within an institutional church, but usually doesn't. So the first arguments are for free church ministry because of the independence of the local church *per se*. The second arguments are for free church ministry as the best place where biblical principles can currently be worked out in practice.

THE INDEPENDENCE OF THE LOCAL CHURCH

As the gospel spreads it leaves churches in its wake. This is the story of the book of Acts. The message of salvation brings people to become Christians through faith in Christ, but more than that it creates churches in the towns and cities where it is preached.

It is clear that in Jerusalem the first church was led by the apostles (see for example Acts 4:34–35). But what about churches where there wasn't an apostle?

The first comment we get on the structure of these churches is in Acts 14 where Paul and Barnabas revisit the places they've preached the gospel:

> **Paul and Barnabas appointed elders for them in each church and, with prayer and fasting, committed them to the Lord, in whom they had put their trust (Acts 14:23).**

The elders here are the local church leaders. The key point to notice is that, having appointed them, Paul and Barnabas committed these churches to the care of God.

We see the same thing when Paul says goodbye to the elders of the church in Ephesus:

> **Now I commit you to God and to the word of his grace, which can build you up and give you an inheritance among all those who are sanctified (Acts 20:32).**

The consistent picture in the New Testament is of local churches having elders appointed to oversee their life and health, and that's all. There's no suggestion of a wider church structure.

This doesn't mean there are to be no relationships between churches. For example, in Acts 11 the church in Antioch heard about a famine that was prophesied to come to Judea, and decided to send financial help to the churches there (Acts 11:27–30). But the key point is that this is what *they* decided to do; there was no outside agency governing them.

A different approach to the same point is to look at the leadership roles described in the New Testament. The most common terms are:

- 'Elders', seen in the passages in Acts above; 1 Timothy 5:17; Titus 1:6; 1 Peter 5:1–4; and elsewhere.
- 'Overseers', seen in Acts 20:28; 1 Timothy 3:1; Titus 1:7; and elsewhere.

These passages demonstrate that the two terms actually describe one position. So in Acts 20 it is the elders from the church at Ephesus whom Paul then calls overseers (see vv. 17 and 28); and in Titus 1 the two words refer to the same position (see vv. 6 and 7). In addition, elders are told to 'oversee' (1 Pet. 5:2).

Another important term used is 'pastor'. This is only used once in Ephesians 4:11. However the action of 'pastoring' is mentioned more frequently, usually translated as 'shepherding'. So the elders / overseers in Acts 20 are told to 'shepherd' or pastor the flock (v. 28). Similarly, the elders in 1 Peter 5 are told to 'oversee' and to 'be shepherds' of the flock (vv. 1–2).

So the usual consensus is that these are three terms

referring to one position: an elder / overseer / pastor. In the New Testament these terms always refer to leading within a single church. The key point then is that there is not another term referring to a leadership role over a number of churches such as a bishop. (The term 'overseer' was traditionally translated 'bishop', but it never referred to a different role.)

So, to recap, the argument for independent churches is:

- Independent churches are what we see described in the New Testament; there is no wider structure described.
- There is only one category of church leader for the local church; there is no additional category of leader who has authority over a number of local churches.

But what about ... ?

Of course those in established church structures have argued back on these points. The arguments for wider structures come from a few places. The following are the most common, to which I have added a brief response.

1. The role of Timothy and Titus

Timothy and Titus are examples of local church leaders but they sometimes seem to exercise greater authority than a local church leader might.

For example, Titus is told to appoint elders on Crete (Tit. 1:5), and Timothy is told not to consider an accusation against a church leader without appropriate witnesses (1 Tim. 5:19–20). Here then, some say, are people acting a bit like a bishop, with roles in overseeing a number of churches to help preserve true doctrine, appoint elders and act as a point of unity.

The difficulty in making this case is two-fold. First, Timothy and Titus act as delegates of Paul and so convey something of his authority as an apostle. That makes them similar to, but different from, the average church leader. Some of their 'authority' may simply be derived from the fact that it is Paul telling them to do things.

Second, it is hard to point to very much that they do which shows *ongoing* authority over churches. The example of Titus appointing elders on Crete is the most obvious, but this is exactly what we might expect in a mission situation where a church has come into being. Paul says that the work on Crete remains unfinished until Titus has done this. Timothy is told how to lead the church in Ephesus (in 1 and 2 Timothy) but there is no indication of any oversight of other churches. Within the leadership of the church in Ephesus itself Timothy is explicitly told about the appointment of other overseers / elders (1 Tim. 3:1–13).

An additional point is that if there were to be ongoing roles like these, we haven't been told about them. Titus is told to appoint elders in each city on Crete but he is not told to appoint someone to oversee all the churches. If Titus' role as an overseer was to continue, why aren't we told about it?

2. The council in Jerusalem in Acts 15

This council comes about because of a dispute raised over whether the Gentiles needed to obey elements of the Old Testament law such as circumcision (Acts 15:1–2). It is often cited by people as an example of a church council or 'synod' with representatives to decide matters on behalf of the whole church. Here then, they argue, is an Anglican synod or Presbyterian council which has authority over local churches. This would indicate a ruling power higher than the local church.

However the council of Acts 15 is not a synod of all the churches because representatives from all the churches are not present. Only Paul and Barnabas go from Antioch to meet with the leaders in Jerusalem (v. 2), which was, at this stage, still the 'mother church'. The decision-making is clearly a corporate activity as we are told that the elders, apostles and whole church are involved (v. 4). But the presence of the apostles complicates things – what sway did they have? Finally the letter they send (vv. 23–29) goes to all the churches but is more by way of advice and encouragement than an official statement that has authority over the churches.

What this council certainly teaches us is the suitability of discussing issues together! Free churches have never been against such councils. What they are against is, first, their necessity – they only think they should happen as they are needed; and, second, their authority – they don't think they have binding authority over all churches.

3. The 'angels' of the churches in Revelation 2–3

This might seem like an odd argument but it has a long history. The word repeatedly used for 'angel', at the start of each letter, simply means messenger, and so the letters from Jesus are given to 'messengers' for each church. This is taken by some to mean an individual leader within each church. Then it is presumed that each city actually has a number of churches and so this leader has an authority over them all, rather like a bishop.

There are lots of assumptions here. First, that the 'messenger' is a real person, because within the imagery of Revelation it may be a way of symbolising communication to each church. Second, that the messenger is a leader rather than simply a messenger. Third, that each of these cities involved a number of congregations over which this person had authority – we simply don't know that that was the case.

LEADERSHIP WITHIN THE LOCAL CHURCH

We've already seen the common terms for church leaders above, and we saw that they are three terms for the same position. We should also note that they are always used in the plural. So free churches have often concluded that each church should be governed by a group of elders. They have sometimes differed as to how this group is organised and whether the 'pastor' is simply one of the elders or has a distinct position. But government by a group of elders working together has been seen as the biblical norm.

In addition, free churches have usually recognised the position of 'deacon'. This is mentioned, along with the elders / overseers, in Philippians 1:1, and the character requirements for deacons are given in 1 Timothy 3. So it is a clear position within the New Testament church. However, we know far less about what deacons actually did. The word simply means 'servant' and so most assume that deacons were officially appointed servants given responsibility for an area of church life under the elders (often seen in Acts 6:1–7).

The result is that most free churches are governed by

a group of elders, often assisted by deacons. One or more of the elders may be employed by the church and referred to as the pastor(s).

Leadership and decision-making in free churches varies a great deal in practice. However common principles would be:

- The respecting and following of the leaders by the congregation (as seen in Heb. 13:17).
- The servant leadership of the leaders in doing what is good for the congregation rather than doing whatever they would like (as seen in 1 Pet. 5:1–4).
- The involvement of the congregation in decision-making (as seen in Acts 6:1–7; Mt. 18:15–17; and 1 Cor. 5:1–5).

How these principles get worked out varies from church to church. Some have a fuller theology of 'congregationalism', where the congregation as a whole is the final authority in the church. This is usually expressed by voting on key decisions. Others are more 'elder-led', with the consultation of the congregation but less (or sometimes no) voting.

At this point some people accuse free churches of being 'unbiblical' in voting! That's a fair point because you can't point to votes in the New Testament. However the involvement of the congregation is very clear. For example, in church discipline, where someone is put out of the fellowship of the church the whole congregation is involved (see Mt. 18:15–17, 1 Cor. 5:1–5 and 2 Cor. 2:6). Voting is not seen as necessary but is a way of embodying this. Free churches will vary in their view of voting: some probably view it wrongly as God's way of speaking; others view it as a way of confirming where the church has got to under the leadership of the elders.

The key point is that all of this is working out biblical teaching on church leadership, structure and decision-making. If this, or something similar, is what you think the Bible teaches on these issues then you will probably want to opt for free church ministry, because that is where you will have the freedom to work out these principles. It is not that they could not be embodied in a national church but simply that they are not currently within the Anglican Church in the UK.

MEMBERSHIP

In addition to leadership positions and decision-making there are other important areas of church life. A key one is what it means to be a member of a local church. The New Testament describes the change that happens between us and God when we are saved, but also the change between us and other Christians. We are united together as a new breed of humanity where Jesus has brought peace between us (Eph. 2:14–16). As a result, Christians in a local church are members of the same family, citizens of the same nation, or bricks in the wall of a new temple (Eph. 2:19–22). Or elsewhere they are different parts of the same body such that we 'belong' to each other (Rom. 12:4–5). This closeness of relationship leads to the responsibilities of membership expressed in the 'one-another' commands – love one another, serve one another, teach one another, encourage one another, accept one another and so on.

This view of membership of the local church can be worked out in different church structures but within free churches there is freedom as to how to do it. It is usually expressed in having a formal membership of some kind. That means there is evaluation of someone's faith and commitment to the church before they become a member (rather than an automatic inclusion on the basis of a parish system or similar). It also means that membership can be made a more meaningful thing, involving deliberate embedding in the life of the church.

This is not to say that free churches always get membership right, because they certainly don't. Rather it is to say that there is, once again, freedom to embody a key aspect of biblical teaching on church life.

BAPTISM

This is not the place to rehearse the arguments for and against baptising the children of believers, or only those who show conscious faith in Christ. But the point is that there are different positions on baptism and that will affect where you can minister. In considering whether to go into the Anglican Church I had to decide whether I could hold a baby in my arms, splash some water on its head, and say, 'I baptise you ...'. If you decide that you think the Bible teaches baptism is only for believers, then you will end up in a free church, because those are the only churches which can hold that position.

BUT DOES THE BIBLE REALLY SPECIFY?

The discussions above have assumed that the Bible gives us the required information to decide how we should govern our churches. But we need to reckon with that issue itself as well. Some people argue that while the New Testament describes the *character* of a church leader in general, it gives none of the specifics of church leadership or structure. A similar claim is that we are not given one version of church leadership, but rather multiple patterns. Others maintain that while we can observe some patterns, none of them are commanded as ongoing for the church throughout history.

If any of these assertions are true, then we should conclude that God has not laid down a pattern for church government. If so, we would then be free to organise ourselves as we think best, in line with general biblical principles. Some say exactly this and so argue that the choice between a free church and an established church can be made on purely pragmatic grounds, that is depending on which one we think works best.

If you do think that, then you still need to consider who gets to make the decisions about the denomination you join. You are agreeing to operate within it and so will have to decide how far you will submit to whatever decision-making authority there is.

However, I would argue that it is not simply a pragmatic decision. Rather, there is one pattern of church leadership clearly observed in the New Testament: local churches led by groups of elders. We have seen some of the important passages above. To summarise:

- Elders are the same as 'overseers' and 'pastors'; these are three terms for one position.
- References to the elders overseeing a church are always in the plural. In particular, we are told that Paul and Barnabas appointed elders (plural) in each church (singular) in Acts 14:23.

- While there are other references to 'leaders' or 'those over you in the Lord', these most naturally refer to those otherwise known as elders (see Heb. 13:17; 1 Thess. 5:12).

So there is one clear pattern. The next question is, 'Is this pattern commanded?' No passage says so directly. We do not read, 'You shall always have elders leading your churches.' However, Paul commanded Titus to appoint elders in Crete and so to complete what had been left unfinished (Tit. 1:5). Paul also gave Timothy the criteria for elders / overseers in 1 Timothy 3:1–7, and clearly expected them to be appointed and functioning in the life of the church. Therefore, the obvious question is, 'If groups of elders were commanded and expected in the first century, why should that have now changed?'

It is true that we do not follow everything we observe about church life in the New Testament. For example we don't feel that we must have lists of widows because they did so in Ephesus (1 Tim. 5:9), even though we take on board the care of widows in our churches. Nor do we specify that money must be put aside on the first day of the week, as Paul advised the Corinthians, since that was for a special collection (1 Cor. 16:2). However, the leadership of elders is a much more persistent theme and seems far more expected in churches than cases like these.

In the end, anyone going into church ministry has to decide: first, what does the Bible specify on areas of church leadership and government?; second, what does it say and not say?; and third, what freedom does that give me as to where I will minister? Good friends of mine have answered those questions and joined the Anglican Church – and they do great good there! Personally, I can only answer those questions by being in a free church context.

A BRIEF HISTORY OF FREE CHURCHES

It is helpful to know something of the history of free churches to appreciate why they came about and how they have organised themselves.

EARLY DISSENT

In the sixteenth century, the Protestant Reformation came to the church in the UK. Most importantly this led to the recapturing of both the gospel of grace and the authority of the Bible. That eventually resulted in the transformation of the national church, in terms of what it taught about salvation and its source of authority.

However, some felt that the Reformation hadn't gone far enough. This lack of complete reformation focused on the following two areas.

First, some thought that the liturgy used in church services wasn't biblical enough, or still contained elements of Roman Catholic thinking. So they wanted the freedom to worship God as they thought the Bible taught and as their conscience required.

Second, others thought that the church structures weren't biblical. They wanted an end to bishops and archbishops. Many wanted church to be led by groups of elders. Some wanted a national church, but where church councils or 'synods' were made up of representatives from local churches (a form of Presbyterianism). Others went further and wanted the independence of the local church.

In addition, there was a third issue for some: that the standard position on baptism was wrong. Rather than baptising infants, they believed you should only baptise those who had come to conscious faith in Christ.

So a variety of new groups were born. They were called 'dissenters' (because they dissented from the national church), or 'nonconformists' (because they refused to conform to it). The different groups were:

- Presbyterians, who still wanted a national church structure rather than independent churches, and who baptised infants.
- Congregationalists, who wanted independent churches but who still baptised infants.
- Baptists, who wanted independent churches and a change in positon on baptism.

PERSECUTION AND FREEDOM

The fortunes of these groups were closely connected to the politics of the day. Dissenting from the national church was seen as a form of civil disobedience, and so dissenters were often punished with fines, imprisonment and even death. Being a religious dissenter and a loyal citizen wasn't a combination many people could conceive of, even though that was exactly what the dissenters themselves were arguing for.

During the Commonwealth, in the seventeenth century, there was a period of freedom for dissenters. The national church of the day became close to being Presbyterian, and there was toleration for other groups. One result of this toleration though, was an explosion of small sects, many of which promoted heretical teaching. For some, this proved that granting freedom only led to anarchy within churches.

The restoration of the monarchy in 1660 saw legislation once again outlawing any dissent from the national church. This resulted in what was called the 'Great Ejection'. Over two thousand ministers left the Church of England because they felt they could not comply with the Prayer Book, would not submit to bishops, or for other reasons. The result was that they joined the ranks of the dissenters.

Dissenters continued to be persecuted until the Toleration Act of 1689. From that point on it has been legal in the UK to dissent from Anglicanism and be part of a 'free church'.

REVIVAL

In the eighteenth century, God revived the church in the UK (as well as in New England and continental Europe). Key leaders in England were the Anglicans George Whitefield and John Wesley. This led to a revived evangelical Anglicanism, but also had an effect on free churches. Some free churches experienced revival directly, resulting in revitalisation and growth. In addition, many new chapels were formed as a result of the revival and a lot of these ended up being independent churches.

NETWORKS AND UNIONS

Towards the end of the eighteenth century, free churches often started working together in new ways. Previously, there had been occasional joint gatherings to debate theological issues and some loose networks; now, these started to be strengthened. For example, the Particular Baptist Missionary Society was formed in 1792, in order for Baptists to partner together to be able to send missionaries overseas.

Later in 1813, a Union of reformed Baptist churches was started. Their aims included overseeing the mission society just mentioned, the training of ministers, financial support for churches, and pensions for the families of deceased ministers.

This type of union showed the ways in which free churches could co-operate together in areas of common concern. However, this was not an institutional denomination: the Union itself had no power over the decisions of the local church. Similar unions were formed for Congregational churches and other Baptist groups.

An important development in the nineteenth century was the start of the Brethren movement. The Brethren brought some distinctive features to church life. They didn't believe in paid, ordained church leaders (which proved to be an unnecessary limitation). But they did believe in the voluntary contribution of congregational members. This helped break the monopoly of the one-man ministry pattern where the minister did everything in the life of the church. They also emphasised the nature of the church as a close-knit community.

Unfortunately, one trend later in the nineteenth century was towards theological liberalism. Key areas of the faith, such as the authority of Scripture, the uniqueness of Christ and the reality of hell were questioned and eventually denied. This affected many churches – both Anglican and free. The free church unions often didn't draw lines where they should have. Rather than having a clear doctrinal basis and only allowing membership of the Union for churches which agreed with it, they relaxed their boundaries. This was seen in the Baptist Union in the 'Down-grade Controversy' where Charles Spurgeon warned of a 'down grade' in theology. The Baptist Union failed to heed his warnings and Spurgeon eventually left the Union.

The desire for independent churches to partner together continued though, and was what lay behind the creation of the FIEC (the Fellowship of Independent Evangelical Churches) in 1922. A minister by the name of Edward Joshua Poole-Conner worked to create an association of 'mutual helpfulness'. One of its key principles was to be united, but only on the basis of the truth of the gospel. The FIEC has grown since then, often being joined by churches leaving groups like the Baptist Union or Brethren networks, as well as by new church plants.

HOW DO FREE CHURCHES WORK IN PRACTICE?

As should be clear by now, this is not an easy question to answer because of the variety of practice between free churches. However, as it might be helpful, this is a description of the most common practice – and the one I would subscribe to!

LEADERSHIP

Leadership is by a group of elders. They meet regularly to pray for the life of the church and its members, to discuss issues and plans, and to decide how to lead the church forward. They are the 'shepherds' of the church who are responsible for its feeding, welfare, and protection (Acts 20:28).

Some of the elders may be employed by the church full-time or part-time, with such elders usually having more theological training and experience. As a result, they usually take responsibility for more of the teaching of the church, such as regular preaching, as well as other responsibilities such as pastoral care and discipleship. However, the paid elders, or pastors, are not 'above' the other elders. They are a team of equals and all elders contribute to the leading of the church.

This 'team leadership' means it takes longer to make decisions than having an individual in charge, but it has so many advantages:

- The corporate wisdom of the group, which is so much greater than that of the individual.
- The complementary gifts and personalities of the group, which lead to more rounded leadership.
- The sharing of ministry tasks, which means so much more can be done and overseen than by one person.
- The mutual encouragement and support, in what can be a hard and lonely task.
- The watching over of each other and keeping each other accountable, rather than there being a lone ranger.

I sleep better at night knowing I lead my church along with a group of elders!

Many free churches also have deacons. They usually take responsibility for a variety of practical areas such as finance or church buildings. In some cases they have a broader remit such as being a deacon for overseas mission, or a deacon for children's work. Sometimes the deacons meet regularly together as a group. In other cases they work more individually and meet with the elders occasionally to discuss their areas of responsibility.

MEMBERSHIP

There is usually a process of becoming a member of the church – rather than simply starting to attend and getting involved. This involves making sure someone is converted (as far as we can tell), that they understand the vision and aims of this church and its ways of working, and that they are committed to being involved in church life. This process can sometimes be unnecessarily cumbersome, but central to it is usually a discussion with one of the elders.

Most churches then have a membership list. This provides a basis for the congregation and the leaders to know who is committed to being part of the church. Of course that should really be anyone who is converted and regularly attending the church, but the process helps people understand what being a member involves. That can be particularly important in a culture that encourages a 'consumer' view of church life.

DECISION-MAKING

Many free churches are well known for having votes. However it is not, or should not be, a democracy. There is a spectrum of decision-making. Some decisions are made by the elders without consulting the congregation. This is actually the majority of decisions in the regular life of the church: services, events, pastoring, evangelism and so on. Then some decisions are made by the elders but with the involvement of the membership by giving suggestions or feedback. Lastly, some decisions are made by a vote of the membership, but even here it is still with the leadership of the elders.

A vote then is a way of confirming where the process has reached. It should be normal for congregations to vote in agreement with a proposal from the elders. However, at this point the elders are genuinely asking the congregation what they think and whether they will give their support. This is usually reserved for the most significant decisions in church life, such as employing a new member of staff, appointing a new elder, or supporting a long-term mission partner. Most churches have a percentage figure (such as two-thirds, or three-quarters) by which such decisions are passed.

LIFE AND MINISTRY

The life and ministry of free churches is many and varied. Central will be the gathering of the church for praise, prayer and preaching. There will often be small groups for study and for looking after and praying for one another. Some free churches have traditions of mid-week prayer meetings or large Bible studies (effectively another sermon), although these are becoming less common. There will also be evangelistic activity, whether in a low-key relational way or through organised events.

In many ways the life and ministry of a free church may look little different to an Anglican Church. But, as we saw earlier, a key feature is that the free church is free to organise their life as they wish. If they'd like to restructure their meetings, they can do so. If they decide they'd be better off meeting as two smaller groups in different locations, they can do so. If they'd like to try to plant a church, there is no permission to ask.

THE ADVANTAGES AND PITFALLS

Let's finish with some of the advantages and potential pitfalls of free church ministry – this will help us sum up what we've seen.

THE ADVANTAGES OF FREE CHURCH MINISTRY

The main advantages of free church ministry revolve around the idea of freedom. As we saw in chapter 1, this is freedom in how they organise their church structure and church ministry, which is wonderfully beneficial.

First, the freedom to organise church life and structure as you and your church want enables you to embody biblical principles in the most appropriate way. This could include:

- Leadership
- Membership
- Church discipline
- Decision-making

For many this is *the* advantage because, as we saw earlier, they have biblical convictions over these areas. It is not so much an advantage as a necessity. This is precisely what led many people to dissent from the established church, because these principles couldn't be worked out there easily, or were even forbidden. The situation has changed today and many Anglicans can work out their convictions happily within the Church of England. However, there is still often the restriction of working within a system, rather than having the freedom to shape church life.

Second, the freedom to exercise ministries as you see fit is what has often given free churches greater flexibility over the years. For example, during the Industrial Revolution new densely populated areas were created in many cities. The free churches had the flexibility to respond to these changes with church planting – often setting up 'Mission Halls' to reach people living in these new housing developments. Anglicans, by comparison, were often constrained by the inflexibility of the parish system. This freedom in starting new churches, and other ministries, means that independent churches today are often those able to lead initiatives in new settings.

Free churches are also free to employ the staff they wish to (assuming they can afford them!), which is not always the case within an institutional church structure. They can appoint leaders within churches without the need for outside recognition. They can have leaders undertake whatever ministries they deem suitable (preaching, leading services, counselling, and so on) rather than having some ministries limited to officially ordained clergy.

In addition, independent churches have the freedom to organise their meetings as they wish rather than having the constraints of an established system which still dictates how some things are to be done. All of this means that free churches are a great place for church ministry today.

THE POTENTIAL PITFALLS OF FREE CHURCH MINISTRY

First, we should acknowledge that good church ministry is not primarily a matter of organisation and structure – these things are the context for ministry, not the heart of ministry. Additionally, good church ministry flows from the godliness, convictions and service of the leaders and the congregation, so we should not think that a well-structured free church is always a healthy church. Ungodliness, heresy, selfishness and much more are just as possible within free churches as anywhere else.

Unfortunately free churches also haven't always taken advantage of the freedoms which are potentially to their advantage. Some have remained stuck with unbiblical or unhelpful leadership structures; they have the freedom to change these, but haven't done so. Some have been rigidly traditional, in the bad sense of perpetuating a past culture and style of ministry; they have the freedom to remain culturally relevant, but haven't taken it. Some have been too conservative, in the negative sense of always taking a safe, well-known option; they have the freedom to take risks in ministry for the sake of the gospel, but they've shied away from them. Some have good structures of leadership with godly elders, but they act too much as 'brakes' on innovations in church life rather than initiators of change; they have the freedom to lead the church forward in accordance with God's word, but have stayed with what was familiar and comfortable. Some have perfectly good decision-making processes, but the congregation has always resisted change.

It is perhaps the tendency to traditionalism that has most hindered free churches. Tradition should always be respected but never bowed to, especially when it is simply the local tradition of how 'we've always done things here'.

Those considering free church ministry need to be aware that they may minister in churches where these issues need facing and changing. However, what these churches need is pastors who will love them, teach them and lead them into the future. And they have the freedom to make that choice.